Insurance in the General Agreement on Trade in Services

AEI STUDIES ON SERVICES TRADE NEGOTIATIONS
Claude E. Barfield, series editor

REDUCING THE BARRIERS TO INTERNATIONAL
TRADE IN ACCOUNTING SERVICES
Lawrence J. White

INSURANCE IN THE GENERAL AGREEMENT ON TRADE IN SERVICES
Harold D. Skipper, Jr.

Insurance in the General Agreement on Trade in Services

Harold D. Skipper, Jr.

The AEI Press

Publisher for the American Enterprise Institute

WASHINGTON, D.C.
2001

Available in the United States from the AEI Press, c/o Publisher Resources Inc., 1224 Heil Quaker Blvd., P.O. Box 7001, La Vergne, TN 37086-7001. To order, call 1-800-937-5557. Distributed outside the United States by arrangement with Eurospan, 3 Henrietta Street, London WC2E 8LU, England.

ISBN 0-8447-7159-7

1 3 5 7 9 10 8 6 4 2

3 6 8
S 6 2 8

The AEI Press
Publisher for the American Enterprise Institute
1150 17th Street, N.W.
Washington, D.C. 20036

Printed in the United States of America

Contents

FOREWORD, *Claude E. Barfield*   V

1   INTRODUCTION   1

2   AN OVERVIEW OF INSURANCE AND
INSURANCE MARKETS   3

3   THE ROLE OF INSURANCE IN ECONOMIC DEVELOPMENT   19

4   OVERVIEW OF THE GATS   26

5   WHAT THE GATS HAS ACCOMPLISHED IN INSURANCE   36

6   WHAT MORE IS NEEDED?   42

7   CONCLUSION   65

NOTES   67

ABOUT THE AUTHOR   71

Foreword

In advanced industrial economies, the service sector accounts for a large majority of each nation's gross domestic product. Yet despite the increasing importance of services trade, the multilateral trading system only began establishing rules to open markets in these sectors in 1995. Against this backdrop the American Enterprise Institute launched a research project to focus on the latest round of international negotiations, Services 2000. The project, mounted in conjunction with the Kennedy School of Government at Harvard, the Brookings Institution, and the U.S. Coalition of Services Industries, will include analyses of individual economic sectors: financial services, accounting, insurance, entertainment and culture, air freight and air cargo, airline passenger service, electronic commerce, and energy. Each study will identify major barriers to trade liberalization in the sector under scrutiny and assess policy options for trade negotiators and interested private-sector participants.

AEI would like to acknowledge the following donors for their generous support of the trade in services project, which provided some of the funding that allowed these studies to go forward: American Express Company, American International Group, Inc., CIGNA Corporation, Enron Corp., FedEx Corporation, Mastercard International Inc., the Motion Picture Association of America, and the

Mark Twain Institute. I emphasize, however, that the conclusions and recommendations of the individual studies are solely those of the authors.

In this monograph, Harold D. Skipper, Jr., of Georgia State University, provides a comprehensive analysis of the insurance industry worldwide and puts forward detailed recommendations for trade rules and regulatory principles that will advance the liberalization of insurance services. While the insurance sector shares many characteristics with banking and securities (treated in a separate monograph in this series), it also demands special attention because of its unique features. In addition, services negotiators have largely ignored this important segment of financial services.

Skipper grounds his later analysis with a clear description of the key elements that make up the insurance industry—life versus other types of insurance, social versus private insurance, and direct insurance versus reinsurance—and adds an overview of the structure of the insurance industry worldwide. Not unexpectedly, the United States and the European Union have by far the largest and most highly developed insurance markets, followed by Japan. Thus, though many developed markets still do not have a large presence of foreign insurers, the most important opportunities for future growth in this industry lie in developing countries.

With this in mind, Skipper next explores the role of insurance in economic development. It is wrong, he argues, to view insurers as merely "pass-through mechanisms for diversifying risk." Important as this function is, it merely "masks other fundamental contributions that insurance makes to prosperity," including promoting financial stability, fostering trade and commerce, enhancing the mobilization of savings, managing risk more efficiently, and improving the efficiency with which capital is mobilized.

Skipper provides a brief description of the General Agreement on Trade in Services (GATS), with special emphasis on those provisions that particularly affect insurance. He also lays out the most important provisions of the supplementary Financial Services Agreement (FSA) adopted in 1998. The FSA, appended to the GATS, established a somewhat deeper level of liberalization, including a binding commitment to grant the right of establishment to foreign corporations and to avoid discrimination in government procurement of financial services. A large percentage of World Trade Organization members committed to at least some elements of liberalization under the FSA, though in many cases they merely agreed to a standstill commitment that bound them to liberalization they had already undertaken domestically. The monograph provides details on the exact nature of these market-access commitments by both developed and developing countries.

The final sections of this study assess what remains to be done and make recommendations with regard to three different goals: generic improvements, liberalized access to markets, and better regulatory principles. On generic improvements, Skipper points to the necessity of advances in rules for government procurement, subsidies, and safeguards, as well as the benefits that would flow from a "negative" list approach for sectoral liberalization and from an across-the-board standstill agreement in GATS. The next steps in market access are obvious and self-explanatory: both developed and developing countries (particularly the latter) need to agree to deeper and more widespread commitments to greater market access for foreign insurance providers. This will only come through point-by-point, detailed negotiations during future full-scale trade rounds.

Finally, the most important issues probably revolve around the creation of procompetitive regulatory rules that allow fully contestable domestic markets among World Trade Organization member states. This can be achieved both through gradual regulatory convergence and also through schemes for mutual recognition of national regulatory systems. In both cases, transparency is indispensable for meaningful cooperation.

Skipper concludes his study by setting forth a model of procompetitive regulatory principles that might form the basis for a separate regulatory annex for insurance—similar to the regulatory annex negotiated as a part of the 1998 Telecommunications Agreement. These principles would embody traits of impartiality, adequate protection of consumers, transparency, and minimal intrusiveness. In fleshing out these traits, governments should enact laws and regulations that provide an effective framework for true domestic competition in insurance, that establish reasonable solvency standards to protect the public, that provide for procedures to identify and deal with financially troubled insurers, that establish an insurance regulatory agency with sufficient resources to enforce national insurance regulations efficiently and impartially, that provide consumer protection while avoiding undue regulatory delay, that limit regulation to minimally intrusive rules, that allow the private sector to determine what insurance products should be developed and how they should be marketed, and that provide full transparency and due process to the public and to the regulated insurers.

One concluding point: in this study as in several of the other sectoral analyses in the series, a call is made for an individual regulatory annex. One of the challenges to the negotiators of upcoming trade rounds will be to decide if, at the end of the day, it makes sense to consolidate all of these sectoral regulatory annexes into one crosscutting document that would lay out procompetitive principles for all of the service sectors covered in the GATS.

CLAUDE E. BARFIELD
American Enterprise Institute

1

Introduction

The General Agreement on Trade in Services (GATS) stands as a monument to the proposition that services can be subject to international trade rules akin to those for goods, and also that the inclusion of services is essential in a world economy increasingly reliant on those services.

GATS now helps structure trade in services around the globe, and it includes all services, providing a framework for future deliberations. At the same time, everyone acknowledges that the financial services part of the agreement represents a patchwork of compromises, as one would expect in so complex an undertaking.

This essay explores how the financial services agreement can be strengthened to promote more competitive, efficient markets that will enhance consumer choice and value and also benefit each country's national interests. The successful conclusion of the financial services agreement on December 12, 1997, brought to a close the often contentious negotiations of two decades to craft reasonable trading rules for services—a goal thought impossible by many, perhaps most, trading partners at the beginning of the Uruguay Round in 1984. The agreement includes commitments from more than 100 countries, which account for more than 95 percent of world trade in financial services. By the end of the extension for the financial services agreement, 70 countries improved their offers.

This assessment of the agreement begins with a general overview of insurance and insurance markets. To provide context for the goal of more efficient insurance markets, I next explore how the insurance industry aids economic development. With this foundation, I then consider the key provisions of the GATS. Finally, I discuss in more detail the accomplishments of GATS regarding insurance and close with ways to overcome the remaining shortcomings.

2

An Overview of Insurance and Insurance Markets

I nsurance exists in every country. Its importance varies with the economic, political, and social conditions of each nation. In general, the more economically advanced a country is, the greater the role played by formal security mechanisms, including insurance. This section explains insurance terminology for readers with little insurance expertise and provides some idea of the importance of insurance worldwide.[1]

Insurance Classifications

Insurance is both a risk-shifting and risk-sharing device. For a consideration (the *premium*), an individual or organization (the *insured*) is guaranteed to be made whole financially by the insuring organization (the *insurer*) if a covered event occurs. The entire scheme functions so long as the insurer is able to insure a sufficient number of similar exposures to keep its overall claims experience reasonably predictable. Generally, the law of large numbers dictates that the greater the number of insureds, the more predictable the insurer's experience.

This comfortably predictable situation may not materialize if the events insured have a catastrophic potential. Also, unforeseen environmental changes can wreck insurers' pricing assumptions; for example, life and health insurers did not anticipate the additional claims AIDS sufferers would bring. In spite of these and many other possible glitches, the world's insurers and reinsurers are largely profitable, stable financial institutions.

Insurance can be classified in many ways, but the following four classifications provide a useful framework:

- Social versus private
- Life versus nonlife
- Retail versus corporate
- Direct insurance versus reinsurance

Social versus Private Insurance. Governments have determined that certain types or minimum levels of insurance coverage are in the nature of public goods. As such, it is held, government—as opposed to the private sector—should provide this cover. Thus, most countries have extensive government-administered social security schemes that provide survivor, retirement, disability, and unemployment benefits. Health insurance and benefits for job-related accidents and illnesses are typically provided by either government or the private sector or some combination of the two.

Social insurance may be distinguished from private insurance through its emphasis on social equity (that is, income redistribution), as contrasted with individual actuarial equity (in which premiums reflect the expected value of losses). Also, participation in social insurance schemes is compulsory, and their financing relies on government-mandated premiums (taxes).

Life versus Nonlife Insurance. The insurance business has historically divided itself between companies that sell insurance on the person, known as *life insurance* (or personal insurance), and those that sell insurance to protect property, referred to as *nonlife insurance*. This classification is not completely satisfactory, as overlaps exist.

The nonlife branch—often referred to as *property/casualty insurance* in the United States and *general insurance* in the United Kingdom—includes insurance that covers (1) property losses (damage to or destruction of homes, automobiles, businesses, aircraft, etc.); (2) liability losses (payments due to professional negligence, product defects, negligent automobile operation, etc.); and, in some countries, (3) workers' compensation (and health insurance) payments.

The life branch includes insurance that pays benefits on a person's (1) death (usually called life insurance or assurance), (2) living a certain period (endowments, annuities, and pensions), (3) disability (disability insurance), and (4) injury or incurring a disease (health insurance). In many markets, notably in Europe, health insurance is classified as nonlife insurance.

The life and nonlife branches of insurance perceive themselves quite differently, with some justification. Many countries prohibit a single corporation from selling both types, although joint production via holding companies and affiliates usually is permitted.

Retail versus Corporate Insurance. Insurance purchased by individuals (homeowners insurance, automobile insurance, individual life insurance, etc.) is often called *retail insurance*. Insurance purchased by businesses and other organizations (product liability, business interruption, automobile insurance, group life insurance, etc.) is often called *corporate insurance*. In some markets, insurance purchased by commercial organizations, especially manufacturing firms, is termed *industrial insurance*.

Direct Insurance versus Reinsurance. Insurance sold to the public and to noninsurance businesses is classified as *direct insurance.* Insurers selling such insurance are called *direct writing* (or *primary*) *insurers* and the attendant premiums are *direct written premiums.*

Insurance purchased by direct writing insurers to hedge their own insurance portfolios is classed as *reinsurance* and is sold by *reinsurers* (with some also sold by the reinsurance departments of direct writing companies). Reinsurance is wholesale insurance. Direct writing companies purchase reinsurance to avoid undue potential loss concentrations, to secure greater underwriting capacity, to stabilize overall financial results, and to take advantage of special expertise possessed by the reinsurer.

Almost all insurers worldwide purchase reinsurance. Reinsurers themselves purchase reinsurance (that is, they *retrocede* business to other reinsurers and the reinsurance departments of direct writing companies). An insurance policy with high payout limits will typically have dozens of insurers and reinsurers sharing the risk on it.

Reinsurance typically involves large exposures to loss, often those with a catastrophic loss potential. As such, the reinsurer must be skillful at underwriting and pricing. As the direct writing company ordinarily is a knowledgeable buyer and the reinsurer is a knowledgeable seller, government intervention into the transaction has historically been nonexistent or kept to a minimum. Reinsurance is probably the most international segment of the insurance business.

Overview of Insurance Worldwide

Insurance markets vary enormously in size and structure. The size of a given country's insurance market depends greatly on the size of its economy, with innumerable environmental influences also shaping its structure. The most commonly accepted measure of insurance market size is gross direct written premiums.[2] Globally, gross direct

Figure 2-1 Life/Nonlife Premium Proportions Worldwide (1997)

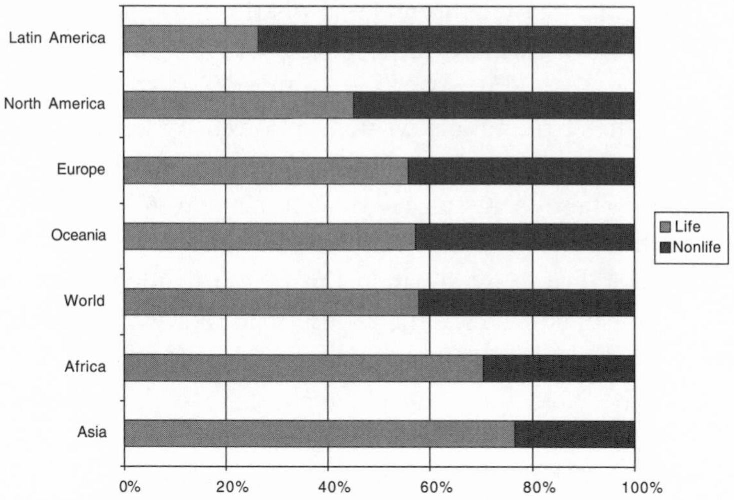

Source: Swiss Re, *sigma*, no. 3 (1999).

written premiums totaled more than $2,100 billion in 1997, having experienced a real average annual growth rate of about 5 percent over the preceding ten years. The south and east Asian, eastern European, and Latin American developing countries have experienced particularly strong development in recent years.

The life sector accounts for 58 percent of world direct premiums, with 42 percent from the nonlife sector.[3] Considerable regional diversity exists in this balance between the life and nonlife sectors, as figure 2-1 suggests. The high proportion of life business for Africa is distorted because of the large South African insurance market, which accounts for 84 percent of African premiums written, with four-fifths of this portion being life premiums. The high Asian propensity to save via life insurance is revealed. Conversely, the adverse effects of past high inflation rates and political instability have historically depressed

Latin American life premium growth, though the situation has changed dramatically for several countries recently.

Figure 2-2 shows the regional distribution of insurance premiums worldwide. North America was the world's largest insurance market in 1997, accounting for 34.5 percent of total direct premiums written, followed by Europe with a 31.4 percent share. Asia's share followed closely at 29.1 percent. These percentages vary from year to year, due primarily to the fluctuation in currency values.

The world's ten largest national markets are shown in figure 2-3. The United States is the largest, followed by Japan, with the United Kingdom, Germany, and France closely bunched thereafter.[4] Note the relatively high share of life business in Japan, France, and Korea. The high share for the two Asian countries results from a high propensity to save, favorable tax treatment, and less developed capital markets. The high French share is attributable to favorable taxation and to successful insurance sales by banks (*bancassurance*).

The Structure of Insurance Markets. National insurance markets have evolved to suit each country's particular environment. The interaction of supply and demand determines their structures. Price and innumerable economic, social, and cultural factors influence the demand for insurance. At the national level, studies consistently find insurance demand to be strongly related to national per capita income.[5] Indeed, these studies consistently show that the income elasticity of insurance tends to be greater than one; that is to say, premium income usually increases at a faster rate than national income.

Higher-income countries purchase more life and nonlife insurance than do lower-income countries. When incomes are low, individuals have little disposable income from which to purchase insurance and fewer assets that justify insurance protection.

Figure 2-2   Distribution of Insurance Premiums Worldwide (1997)

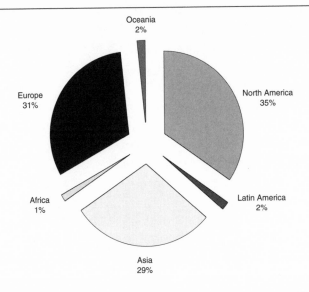

Source: Swiss Re, *sigma*, no. 3 (1999).

Figure 2-3   Ten Largest Insurance Markets (1997) in $ billions

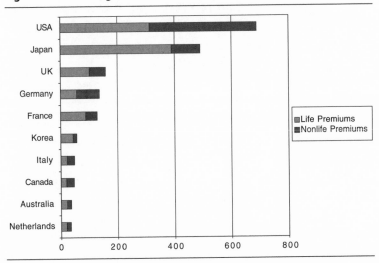

Source: Swiss Re, *sigma*, no. 3 (1999).

As economic development increases, incomes and assets rise as well, as do demand to protect them and the money to pay premiums. Additionally, informal insurance arrangements such as the extended family become increasingly less able to offer sufficient security as families shrink in size, become more geographically dispersed, and are more dependent on employment income. Informal arrangements give way to formalized economic security efforts, such as social insurance programs, employer-provided security, and individually purchased private insurance.

The two most prevalent forms of insurers worldwide are stocks and mutuals. *Stock insurers* are owned by shareholders, with profits accruing to them. *Mutual insurers* have no shareholders; they are effectively owned by the policyholders to whom their profits flow. The stock insurer form predominates in most lines and markets worldwide. Mutuals control important market shares in France, Japan, and the United States.

The world's largest insurers are located in the more advanced countries. Table 2-1 lists the world's twenty-five largest insurers, based on revenues, along with their countries of domicile and their legal form. The table also indicates whether the insurance company (or group) is engaged principally in the life or nonlife business. As a practical matter, most insurers operate in groups and engage in both the life and nonlife businesses.

By this measure, the United States is home to eight of the top twenty-five insurers, Japan is second with six, and the United Kingdom is third with three. Most of the insurers listed in table 2-1 write the majority of their business within their domestic markets.

The International Dimensions of Insurance. With the increasing internationalization of business comes a corresponding internationalization of financial services.

Table 2-1 World's Largest Insurance Companies, by Revenues, 1998

Rank	Company	Country of Domicile	Type of Insurer (Principal Line*)	1998 Revenues ($ millions)
1	AXA	France	Stock (L/H)	78,729
2	Nippon Life	Japan	Mutual (L/H)	66,300
3	Allianz	Germany	Stock (P/C)	64,875
4	ING Group	Netherlands	Stock (L/H)	56,469
5	Assicurazioni Generali	Italy	Stock (P/C)	48,478
6	State Farm	USA	Mutual (P/C)	44,621
7	Dai-ichi Mutual Life	Japan	Mutual (L/H)	44,486
8	Sumitomo Life	Japan	Mutual (L/H)	39,535
9	Zurich Financial	Switzerland	Stock (P/C)	39,115
10	CGNU	UK	Stock (P/C)	37,589
11	TIAA-CREF	USA	Mutual (L/H)	35,889
12	Munich Re Group	Germany	Stock (P/C)	35,465
13	Prudential of America	USA	Stock (L/H)**	34,427
14	Prudential (UK)	UK	Stock (L/H)	33,677
15	American Int'l Group	USA	Stock (P/C)	33,296
16	Meiji Mutual Life	Japan	Mutual (L/H)	28,476
17	Metropolitan Life	USA	Stock (L/H)**	26,735
18	Allstate	USA	Stock (P/C)	25,879
19	Royal & Sun Alliance	UK	Stock (P/C)	25,436
20	CNP Assurances	France	Stock (L/H)	24,108
21	Mitsui Mutual Life	Japan	Mutual (L/H)	22,226
22	Leows	USA	Stock (P/C)	20,713
23	New York Life	USA	Mutual (L/H)	19,849
24	Asahi Mutual Life	Japan	Mutual (L/H)	19,418
25	Aegon	Netherlands	Stock (L/H)	18,727

*L/H = life and health insurance; P/C = property and casualty (nonlife) insurance.
**Demutualization in process.
Source: Jeremy Kahn, "The Fortune Global 500," *Fortune*, August 2, 1999.

Additionally, the size and concentration of many purely domestic loss exposures require a mustering of international insurance capacity. No one country's market can provide needed cover for property and liability loss exposures arising from oil refineries, tankers, offshore rigs, satellites, jumbo jets, environmental impairment, and the like. An international spread is essential if such large risks are to be insured.

Reinsurance is particularly important in this regard. The large reinsurance companies—such as Munich Re (Germany), Swiss Re (Switzerland), General Re (United States), and SCOR (France)—conduct substantial international operations that augment national insurance capacity.

Perhaps fewer than a dozen direct writing insurers are truly international, capable of servicing their customers worldwide. Among such firms are the American International Group, CIGNA, and Chubb in the United States; the Royal & Sun Alliance and CGNU in the United Kingdom; AXA in France; the Zurich in Switzerland; and Allianz in Germany. Dozens of other insurers have important foreign operations or seek such operations. For many insurers, international expansion provides a valuable means of achieving additional growth when their domestic markets are saturated, as in America.

Of course, national markets can benefit from a greater international insurance and reinsurance presence that increases the domestic supply of insurance and thereby enhances competition and provides better consumer value and choice. As with other international operations, knowledge-sharing can bring innovation: new products, production and underwriting techniques, and claims-settling practices. Increasing competition and innovation in insurance also enhances the international competitiveness of domestic insurance firms.

Foreign interests can deliver insurance services through either cross-border trade or establishment. *Cross-border insurance trade* exists when the buyer purchases (imports) insurance from an insurer or reinsurer domiciled in another country; for example, a Ghanaian corporation (importer) purchases insurance directly from a U.K. insurer (exporter). Delivery via *establishment insurance trade* exists when the buyer purchases insurance from a domestic, foreign-owned entity. The foreign presence may come via a local agent with authority to underwrite business on the foreign insurer's behalf, or through a branch office of an international firm, or through the creation or purchase of a local insurer or reinsurer by an international provider.

Because data on the dimensions of international insurance supply are sparse, assessing its size and importance is difficult. Most national accounting systems fail to make appropriate allowance for insurance and reinsurance trade (though the United Kingdom is an important exception). Additionally, classification problems exist with trade-related insurance, such as marine insurance—a particularly important line in many countries.

Cross-border Insurance Trade. Cross-border trade in life insurance is believed to be quite small, probably less than 1 percent of world premiums. Cross-border trade in nonlife insurance worldwide is believed to account for less than 5 percent of such premiums, with the great majority being reinsurance and commercial insurance, including particularly marine, aviation, and transport insurance (known as MAT insurance).

Cross-border insurance trade can take several forms. *Pure cross-border insurance trade* exists when the resultant insurance contract is entered into because of solicitation by a foreign insurer. The solicitation may have come via direct response techniques (telephone, newspaper, mail, Internet, etc.) or brokers. Such insurance typically involves large risks. Much reinsurance is marketed in this way.

Own-initiative cross-border insurance trade occurs when the insured initiates contact with the insurer. Corporations often seek insurance abroad in hopes of securing more favorable terms, conditions, or prices than those available locally. Individuals less frequently do so. One should make a further distinction between such own-initiative insurance in which the insured has no relationship with the insurer and that where the insured owns the foreign insurer (a so-called captive insurer).

Consumption-abroad cross-border insurance trade occurs when an insured entity, temporarily resident or visiting abroad, enters into an insurance contract with a local insurer. A further distinction is made between such purchases intended to provide cover only during the original stay and insurance that provides longer-term coverage.

The United States has a hybrid of cross-border insurance trade known as *surplus lines insurance*. Most U.S. jurisdictions prohibit pure cross-border trade. Only after being denied desired coverage in the admitted market (that is, from licensed insurers) may the proposed insured seek insurance from nonadmitted (unlicensed, surplus lines) insurers. Such insurance is placed through specially licensed domestic brokers.

We see another variation of cross-border insurance trade when a multinational enterprise (MNE) purchases *difference-in-conditions insurance* or *difference-in-limits insurance* as part of its global risk-management program. Such policies, usually written in the MNE's home country, may involve coinsurance with foreign or other domestic insurers. Coverage may extend to many exposures of the parent and its foreign affiliates. Affiliates often purchase underlying insurance locally, with the master contract providing excess or gap coverage.

Establishment Insurance Trade. National insurance markets are typically composed of some combination of domestic and foreign insurers. A *domestic insurer* is one domiciled (incorporated) in the concerned country. Except in the United States, a *foreign insurer* is one domiciled in another country.[6] An insurer's country of domicile is its *home country*. The country in which an insurer conducts business as a foreign insurer is its *host country*.

Important differences exist in establishment by agency, branch, subsidiary, and representative office. An *agency* is a representative of an insurer and typically performs the distribution and possibly underwriting and claim-settlement functions only. It is not a risk-bearing entity. The agency neither holds nor manages any insurer assets. Payments to claimants must come from funds held by the insurer in its home country. This form of establishment closely resembles cross-border trade with the principal regulatory responsibility resting with the home-country supervisor, except for marketing practices.

Branches represent a more substantial form of establishment because assets to back local reserves are usually maintained in the host country. Governments often require local deposits equal to minimum capital and surplus requirements. Nonetheless, branches are not separate corporations. They are a part of the home-country insurer. As such, they are subject to dual regulatory oversight, which can create problems.

Establishment by purchasing or creating a subsidiary poses far fewer policy issues. A *subsidiary* is a company owned by another company. The local subsidiary of a foreign insurer is a domestic corporation, fully subject to host country laws and regulation. Often, subsidiaries are created as *joint ventures* between a foreign insurer and a local corporation.

As a fourth form of establishment, a *representative office* seeks to promote the interests of and sometimes services the local clients of the foreign insurer. The representative office neither bears risk nor sells insurance. Within the thirty industrialized countries that make up the Organization for Economic Cooperation and Development (OECD), establishment requires host country regulatory notification but not approval.

Each form of establishment usually involves employment of home country nationals. This employment may be temporary or longer term, depending on the foreign insurer's philosophy and mode of operations as well as on the experience, skills, and talents of host country nationals.

Precise international insurance establishment trade figures are not available. Globally perhaps 10 percent of nonlife premiums and 5 percent of life premiums are written by foreign insurers through local establishment, and the percentages are growing. The extent of foreign presence within domestic insurance markets varies greatly worldwide, from nil within previously closed markets such as India to more than 30 percent in Canada, Austria, and Australia. Figures 2-4 and 2-5 provide data for foreign market shares of life and nonlife insurance within selected OECD countries.

Foreign insurance firms' success within a market varies with the market's structure. Foreign firms traditionally have been most successful in the more complex insurance lines, such as commercial insurance, MAT insurance, and reinsurance. Their typically large size, geographic spread of risk, in-depth knowledge of complex risks, and management efficiency have enabled them to compete successfully with local firms. With important exceptions, domestic firms dominate the less complex personal lines and life insurance.

The pace of mergers and acquisitions among cross-border financial service firms has been particularly brisk during the past ten years. The European Union Single Market program

Figure 2-4 Foreign Insurers' Market Share for Selected OECD Countries: Life Premiums, 1996

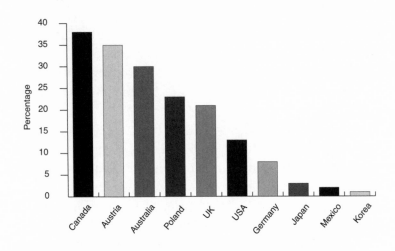

Source: OECD.

Figure 2-5 Foreign Insurers' Market Share for Selected OECD Countries: Nonlife Premiums, 1996

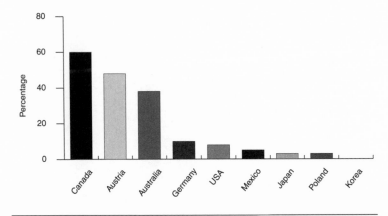

Source: OECD.

has resulted in a significant number of European mergers and acquisitions. Most transactions are intra-European, although many European firms have acquired important U.S. insurers and reinsurers.

Establishment within certain markets is particularly difficult. Besides government-created impediments to entry, certain market structures also create impediments. Japan has been the object of particularly intense interest in this regard.

Regulatory transparency has also been a problem for firms seeking entry into some other insurance markets. Some countries traditionally allow their officials great latitude and so their insurance laws and regulations are written in general terms, with interpretation left to administrative guidance. As a result, a foreign insurer may be unable to know specific entry requirements in advance and unable to learn readily whether it is being treated the same way domestic firms are. Also, the absence of detailed written standards can hinder foreign insurers' ability to question or challenge arbitrary or unreasonable actions by the regulator. Numerous countries have recently taken steps to render their regulation more transparent and to ensure more open, competitive markets.

3

The Role of Insurance
in Economic Development

Promoting the liberalization of international financial
services trade is a worthy goal because insurance provides invaluable aids to economic development.[1] The
more developed and efficient a country's insurance market,
the greater will be its contribution to economic prosperity.

Insurers are not simple pass-through mechanisms for
diversifying risk under which the unfortunate few who suffer losses are indemnified from the funds collected from
many insureds. Laudable though this function is, it masks
other fundamental contributions that insurance makes to
prosperity. Countries that best harness these contributions
give their citizens and businesses greater economic opportunities. Insurance provides seven categories of services
important to economic growth.

Insurance Can Promote Financial Stability. Insurance
helps stabilize the finances of individuals, families, and
organizations by indemnifying those who suffer loss or
harm. Without insurance, individuals and families could
become financially destitute and forced to seek assistance
from relatives, friends, or the government. Businesses that
incur significant uninsured losses may suffer major reverses
or even fail. In such cases, not only the loss in value of the

owners' stake in the business is forgone, but also the firm's future contribution to the economy: employees lose jobs, suppliers lose business, customers lose the opportunity to buy from the firm, and government loses tax revenues. The stability provided by insurance encourages individuals and firms to create wealth with the assurance that their resources can be protected.

Insurance Can Substitute for and Complement Government Security Programs. Insurance, especially life insurance, can substitute for government security programs. Private insurance also complements public security programs. It can thus relieve pressure on social welfare systems and allow individuals to tailor their security programs to their own preferences. Studies have confirmed that greater private expenditures on life insurance are associated with a reduction in government expenditures on social insurance programs.[2] This substitution role is especially valuable given the growing financial challenges faced by national social insurance systems.

Insurance Can Facilitate Trade and Commerce. Many products and services are produced and sold only if adequate insurance is available. Insurance coverage is a condition for engaging in some activities. Because of the high risk of new business failure, venture capitalists often make funds available only if tangible assets and the entrepreneurs' lives are adequately insured. Entrepreneurs are more likely to create and expand their business ventures if they can secure adequate insurance protection. Insurance underpins much of the world's trade and entrepreneurial activity.

This fact is unsurprising. Modern economies are built on specialization and its inherent productivity improvements. Greater trade and commercial specialization demand, in turn, greater financial specialization and flexibility. Without a wide choice of insurance products and constant service and pricing innovations, insurance inadequacies could stifle both trade and commerce. In these ways insurance serves as "a lubricant of commerce."

Insurance Can Help Mobilize Savings.   Studies have shown that, on average, countries that save more tend to grow faster.[3] Insurers play an important role in channeling savings into domestic investment. Insurers enhance the efficiency of financial systems in three ways. First, insurers reduce transaction costs associated with bringing together savers and borrowers. Thousands of individuals each pay relatively small premiums, and insurers then invest these funds as loans to businesses and other ventures. When insurers perform this intermediation function, they help individual policyholders avoid the costly, time-consuming tasks of direct lending and investing. Insurers can acquire the information necessary to make sound investments more efficiently than individuals can. In turn, the efficiencies and higher returns achieved by insurers are passed on to policyholders as lower premiums.

Second, insurers create liquidity. Insurers invest the funds entrusted to them by their customers to make long-term loans and other investments. Policyholders, however, have immediate access to loss payments and savings, while borrowers need not repay their loans immediately. If all individuals instead undertook equivalent direct lending, the proportion of their personal wealth held in long-term, illiquid assets would be unacceptably high. Insurers and other financial intermediaries thereby reduce the illiquidity inherent in direct lending.

Third, insurers facilitate economies of scale in investment. Many investment projects are quite large, especially in relation to the financial capital available in many emerging markets. By amassing large sums from thousands of smaller premium payers, insurers can often meet the financing needs of such large projects, which in turn helps the national economy by enlarging the set of feasible investment projects and encouraging economic efficiency. For example, insurers in the United States provide financing for fully one-third of all corporate debt.

A well-developed financial system will have myriad financial institutions and instruments. Other things being equal, the greater the variety of financial institutions and products, the more efficient the system and the greater its contribution to economic development. Contractual savings institutions, such as life insurers and private pension funds, can be especially important financial intermediaries in emerging markets. In contrast with commercial banks, which often specialize in collecting short-term deposits and extending short-term credit, contractual savings institutions usually take a longer view. Their longer-term liabilities and stable cash flows are ideal sources of long-term finance for government and business.

Insurance Can Enable Risk To Be Managed More Efficiently. Financial systems and intermediaries price risk and provide for risk transformation, pooling, and reduction. The better that a nation's financial system provides these various risk-management services, the greater the saving and investment stimulation and the more efficiently resources are allocated.

Risk pricing. A competitive market's success depends on pricing. The pricing of risk is fundamental to all financial intermediaries and is no less important to their resource allocation than to any other supplier of goods or services.

Insurers price risk at two levels. First, insurers evaluate the loss potential of businesses, persons, and property for which they might provide insurance. The greater the expected loss potential, the higher the price. In pricing loss

potential, insurers cause insureds to quantify the conse-
quences of their risk-causing and risk-reduction activities
and thus more rationally deal with risk. Investors in projects
judged too risky for insurance at any price are put on notice
and should rationally expect returns commensurate with the
risk. When governments interfere with accurate insurance
pricing, their actions can distort the allocation of insurance
and, consequently, other resources.

Second, insurers evaluate the creditworthiness of those to
whom they extend loans and the likely business success of
those in whom they invest. This process helps business
owners, potential investors, customers, creditors, employees, and other stakeholders to be better informed about the
firm's risk characteristics.

Risk transformation. Insurance permits businesses and
individuals to transform their risk exposures to suit their
needs better. Many property, liability, loss of income, and
other risk exposures can be transferred to an insurer for a
price, and in the process the insured's risk profile is
changed. In addition, by tailoring contracts to the needs of
different clients, life insurers help individuals and businesses transform the characteristics of their savings to the
liquidity, security, and risk profile desired.

Risk pooling and reduction. Risk pooling and reduction lie
at the heart of insurance and, as with risk pricing, occur at
two levels. First, in aggregating many individual risk exposures, insurers can make reasonably accurate estimates of
the pool's aggregate losses. The larger the number of
insureds, the more stable and predictable is the insurer's
experience. This fact leads to a reduction in volatility and
thus permits insurers to charge smaller risk premiums for
uncertainty and maintain more stable premiums.

Second, insurers benefit from pooling through their
investment activities. By providing funds to a broad range
of enterprises and individuals, insurers diversify their

investment portfolios. The default of a few borrowers is likely to be offset by many sound investments. The more stable and predictable an insurer's investment experience, the less it can charge for loans.

Insurance Can Encourage Loss Mitigation. Insurance companies have economic incentives to help insureds to prevent and reduce losses. Moreover, their detailed knowledge about loss-causing events, activities, and processes gives them a competitive advantage over many other firms in loss assessment and control. When the pricing or availability of insurance is tied to loss experience and risky behavior, insureds, in turn, have economic incentives to control losses.

Insurers support many loss-control programs, including fire prevention; occupational health and safety activities; industrial loss prevention; reduction in automobile damage, theft, and injury; and literally dozens of other loss-control activities and programs. These programs and activities reduce losses to businesses and individuals and complement good risk management. Society as a whole benefits from the reduction of such losses.

Insurance Can Foster Efficient Capital Allocation. Insurers gather substantial information to evaluate firms, projects, and managers both in deciding whether and at what price to issue insurance and also in their roles as lenders and investors. Individual savers and investors may not have the time, resources, or ability to undertake this information gathering and processing, but insurers have an advantage in this regard and are better at allocating financial capital and insurance risk-bearing capacity. Insurers will choose to insure and to provide funds to the soundest and most efficient firms, projects, and managers.

Insurers have a continuing interest in and monitor the firms, projects, and managers to whom they provide financial capital and risk-bearing capacity. They encourage managers and entrepreneurs to act in the best interests of their various stakeholders (customers, stockholders, creditors, etc.). By doing so, insurers tangibly signal the market's approval of promising, well-managed firms and foster a more efficient allocation of a country's scarce financial capital and risk-bearing capacity. National financial systems that impose minimum constraints on insurers' abilities to gather and evaluate information in this way should enjoy a more efficient allocation of capital and therefore stronger economic growth.

4

Overview of the GATS

The General Agreement on Trade in Services (GATS) is
a part of the Agreement Establishing the World Trade
Organization (WTO), and it laid down the first-ever
set of multilateral, legally enforceable rules covering international trade in services. It follows the companion General
Agreement on Tariffs and Trade (GATT) in key respects, but
deviates from it in important ways. The GATS operates at
three levels:

- The framework agreement sets out general principles
  and obligations.
- Annexes contain rules for specific service sectors.
- Schedules list each signatory country's specific commitments and exemptions.

The Framework Agreement

The GATS's twenty-nine articles cover all service sectors. They
define modes of supply of services and contain the general
obligations and specific commitments of member countries.

Modes of Supply. Trade in services is defined in Article I in
terms of four modes of supply: (1) *Cross-border*, in which
the buyer and supplier are domiciled in different countries.
This mode is closest to international trade in goods because
the service crosses a border. Reinsurance and MAT insurance

are commonly sold cross-border. (2) *Consumption abroad,* in which the buyer purchases the service while in another country. This mode, a variation of cross-border, is not of great importance in terms of premiums written internationally. (3) *Establishment of a commercial presence* in another country in which the insurer purchases a subsidiary or creates a branch or subsidiary. This mode is the most important in insurance. (4) *Temporary presence of a citizen* from one country in another country for purposes of rendering services there; for example, a British actuary provides advice in Kenya. This mode is the least important to insurance.

Establishment, of course, requires foreign direct investment either to purchase an existing company or to capitalize a new one. By including this mode, the GATS differs from the GATT, which does not deal with international trade via foreign direct investment. International trade in many services requires a commercial presence, whereas trade in goods generally does not; hence, the inclusion of this mode in the GATS.

Services supplied in the "exercise of governmental authority" are not covered under the GATS. The definition includes "any service which is supplied neither on a commercial basis, nor in competition with one or more services suppliers." The annex later makes clear that the GATS's obligations do not apply to such services. Thus, any social security or public retirement plans are excluded, unless the government allows private service providers to compete with the public plan.

General Obligations and Disciplines. The GATS framework agreement contains two important general obligations: most favored nation treatment (MFN) and transparency.[1] With the exceptions noted below, member countries are bound to honor these two obligations in all service sectors.

The general MFN obligation in the GATS (Article II) is similar to what is found in the GATT. It requires signatory governments to avoid discrimination among trading partners; that is, to accord no country treatment less favorable than that accorded to the most favored country. As with the GATT, allowances are included for preferential trade agreements, provided they meet certain conditions (Article V). Members are permitted to take exemptions for specific measures, but only with respect to initial commitments and only at time of entry into force of the GATS. Such exemptions are subject to negotiation and, in principle, are to last no longer than ten years.

The other general obligation (Article III), from which no exemptions are permitted, is transparency. Governments are required to publish all laws, regulations, and administrative guidelines relevant to services trade. They must establish inquiry points whereby other members can obtain needed regulatory information. The World Trade Organization must be notified of new laws, regulations, and guidelines, or changes in existing ones, "which significantly affect trade in services" encompassed in a country's specific commitments.

Several other provisions of the General Obligations and Disciplines warrant mention. First, Article VI, "Domestic Regulation," is important, perhaps more for the principle of its being in the agreement than for its requirements. Paragraph 1 provides that, for sectors for which specific obligations are undertaken, members shall ensure that domestic regulations "are administered in a reasonable, objective and impartial manner." Members must provide an impartial means of reviewing administrative decisions. If authorization is required to supply a service, as in insurance, for which specific commitments are made, the responsible agency is to inform applicants "within a reasonable period of time" of its decision.

Measures involving qualification requirements, technical standards, and licensing procedures are to be based on objective and transparent criteria that are no more burdensome than necessary to ensure the quality of the concerned service and that do not, in themselves, constitute restrictions on market access or national treatment.

The agreement in Article IX recognizes that certain nonmonopoly business practices can restrain competition and thereby restrict trade in services. Members are required to "enter into consultations with a view to eliminating" such practices identified by other members. This requirement includes providing any publicly available information relevant to a competition matter to other members, if requested. This article, however, imposes no obligations on members regarding the existence or enforcement of competition policy.

Specific Commitments. Unlike the general obligations, specific commitments do not apply to all services, but only to those sectors listed in a country's schedule of commitments, and then only to the extent further limitations are not invoked. The shortcomings associated with this so-called conditional positive list ("bottom-up") approach have been documented, as have the explanations for its use.[2]

Specific commitments are made on market access and national treatment. Members may also inscribe additional commitments. Collectively these commitments constitute the core of the GATS. The dedication of a country to liberalization can be inferred from the quality of its schedule of commitments.

Procedurally, members first decide which service sectors and modes of delivery within each sector will be subject to the market-access obligation. For sectors inscribed in member schedules, the national-treatment obligation applies, except for any inscribed conditions. Members then decide which measures inconsistent with the obligations will, nonetheless, be retained. Thus, members schedule their commitments as follows:

- *No commitment*—no obligations concerned with market access or national treatment are made; the entry designation is "unbound" [3]
- *Commitments with limitations*—the limitations are measures inconsistent with obligations to market access or national treatment
- *Full commitment*—full obligations to market access or national treatment are made; the entry designation is "none" or "no limitations"

Market Access. The GATT does not contain a general right of market access. Instead of a definition of market access, the GATS (Article XVI) prohibits limitations on

1. the number of suppliers
2. the total value of service transactions or assets, including economic-needs tests
3. the total number of service operations or the total quantity of service output, including economic-needs tests
4. the total number of naturalized persons who may be employed
5. the types of legal entities through which a service supplier may supply a service
6. participation of foreign capital

This list is not exhaustive. An important omission is fiscal measures. A country could, for example, maintain a discriminatory tax on insurance premiums written by foreign insurers without violating the market-access obligation, even if the country's schedule of insurance commitments were fully bound for all modes of supply.

Unless a mode of supply within a sector is unbound, member countries must indicate in their schedules the extent to which any of the above six restrictions apply for each mode of supply. The first and sixth limitations remain prominent in insurance.

A right of market access is fundamental to the provision of many services, including insurance. Ideally, market access would encompass the right of the service provider to enter a market through the mode of its choosing, but the GATS does not establish such a right. Of course, the market-access right must be activated by having the service sector listed in the member's schedule of commitments, and, even if it is listed, inconsistent measures can be retained.

National Treatment. The GATS national-treatment obligation (Article XVII) requires members to treat foreign services and service suppliers no less favorably than similar domestic services and suppliers. Either identical or different treatment is permitted, provided the resultant "conditions of competition" do not favor domestic services or service providers.

This GATS obligation is wider in scope than the analogous obligation in the GATT because it applies to both cross-border and establishment trade, whereas the GATT applies only to the former. At the same time, however, its application is more limited. The GATT's national-treatment obligation follows a negative list ("top-down") approach. With a hybrid positive list approach, the GATS's obligation is limited only to those sectors listed by members in their schedules, and exemptions are allowed from those.

Additional Commitments. Article XVIII provides a mechanism for signatories to make additional commitments beyond those enumerated under the market-access and national-treatment provisions. Additional commitments must offer more open markets; they cannot lead to more restrictive markets. They may relate to such matters as qualifications, standards, and licensing.

This article proved quite useful in the December 1997 negotiations. The United States and the European Union wanted Japan to bind within the GATS its 1994 and 1996 bilateral insurance agreements with the United States. Arguing that those agreements applied to domestic regulation and not to trade matters, Japan at first demurred. Ultimately, Japan agreed to include the agreements' provisions under the additional commitments article, but only after the European Union and America agreed to schedule as additional commitments their promise to undertake their "best endeavours" at future domestic deregulation, including state regulatory harmonization in the case of the United States.[4]

Several countries have used this article to record their future commitments to further liberalization. In effect, this article helps bring domestic regulatory issues within the ambit of the GATS.

The Annex on Financial Services

The GATS annexes (Article XXIX) reflect some of the diversity of services. The financial services annex contains several provisions, among which these four are particularly important in insurance:

- prudential carve-out
- recognition of prudential measures
- dispute settlement
- definitions

Prudential Carve-out. Given the nature of financial services, some method of allowing governments to avoid having their legitimate regulation classified as a trade barrier was essential to successful GATS negotiations. As a result, the agreement excludes prudential domestic regulation:

> Notwithstanding any other provision of the Agreement, a Member shall not be prevented from taking measures for prudential reasons, including for the protection of investors, depositors, policy holders or persons to whom a fiduciary duty is owed by a financial service supplier, or to ensure the integrity of the financial system.

The same section prohibits this provision from being used to avoid other commitments or obligations under the agreement. Prudential measures need not be inscribed in members' schedules of commitments.

The prudential carve-out is broadly worded. In fact, the annex contains neither a definition nor examples of prudential measures. In addition, the annex does not require that measures be no more burdensome than necessary to accomplish their purpose. Disputes as to whether a measure qualifies for this exemption are subject to dispute settlement.

Recognition of Prudential Measures. Article VII of the framework agreement allows members to recognize the licenses or other requirements of members not dealt with under the market-access and national-treatment provisions. The annex effectively extends this provision by allowing a member to recognize prudential measures of one or more members without being subject to challenge by other members. Typically, mutual recognition would be the approach, but the provision applies equally to unilateral recognition. Other members meeting the same standard must be accorded like recognition.

Dispute Settlement. As a compromise to the concerns of many national financial services regulators, provision is made for disputes involving prudential and other financial matters to be delegated to a dispute-settlement panel with expertise specific to the financial service in question. Other provisions within the World Trade Organization context specify that, if retaliation is appropriate, it must proceed in this order: first, against the sector in dispute; second, against other services sectors if the first is not feasible; and third, against any other sector (for example, goods) if the second is not feasible.

Definitions. The annex contains this definition of a financial service: "any service of a financial nature offered by a financial service supplier of a member. Financial services include all insurance and insurance-related services, and all banking and other financial services (excluding insurance)."

A listing of activities that fall within the insurance and related category follows, as well as a list of activities that fall within the banking and other financial services category. The insurance category includes

- direct insurance, both life and nonlife
- reinsurance and retrocession
- insurance intermediation, such as brokerage and agency
- services auxiliary to insurance, such as consultancy, actuarial, risk assessment, and claim-settlement services

Many observers contend this listing is less complete than desirable. They note that it may not be clear that certain types of insurance—such as title insurance, surety, and pensions—are included.

The Understanding on Commitments in Financial Services

Several countries, including almost all OECD members and a few developing countries, undertook commitments through the Understanding on Commitments in Financial

Services. The Understanding, appended to the GATS, effectively substitutes a greater level of liberalization for countries that schedule their commitments there. The Understanding includes a commitment not to enact new, nonconforming measures and also requires members to permit cross-border trade of selected financial activities, including MAT insurance, reinsurance and retrocession, and services auxiliary to insurance.

Members are also bound to grant a right of establishment and to avoid discrimination in government procurement of financial services. Importantly, the Understanding requires members to permit established foreign suppliers of financial services to offer any new financial service. Members who schedule their commitments through the Understanding are not, however, obligated to accept all of its provisions, and several have inscribed limitations.

5

What the GATS Has Accomplished in Insurance

If one measured the progress of the GATS by examining the differences in commitments between those in the 1993 Final Act and the 1997 Financial Services Agreement, a proclamation of success would be in order. Some seventy countries improved their offers, many substantially so.

Much of this improvement, however, cannot be fairly attributed to negotiations involving the GATS. Numerous countries had undertaken insurance reform and liberalization during the period, independent of the GATS, after concluding correctly that it was in their national interests. As a result, most member countries effectively bound what was (or was to become) their status quo in 1997, but relatively few made new commitments to liberalization.

This result, however, is not to be discounted. For one thing, most countries that had undertaken market liberalization and deregulation actions prior to the finalization of the GATS committed to maintaining these positions. For another, it is important to have a baseline from which future negotiations can proceed.

What is the nature of commitments worldwide? In the following overview of commitments, I draw heavily from the work of Aaditya Mattoo and R. Brian Woodrow, both of whom have thoughtfully examined the nature of members' insurance commitments.[1] Mattoo's study focused on the market-access commitments in direct insurance for 105 developing and transition economies. Woodrow drew general observations across all signatory countries as relates to national treatment and market access commitments.

The OECD Countries. Woodrow summarized the commitments made by OECD countries:

- all made full bindings for market access and national treatment, subject to specific limitations
- commercial presence was clearly the favored mode of supply for life and nonlife insurance
- commercial presence and cross-border trade were accepted by the great majority of countries in the fields of insurance intermediation and auxiliary services
- full cross-border trade and consumption abroad in life and nonlife insurance are the exception rather than the rule
- limitations on market access and national treatment are more widespread and substantial in life and nonlife insurance than other activities
- the great majority of countries inscribed no limitations on the number of suppliers or on equity participation, although many placed limitations on the legal form that commercial presence may take
- all but Korea and Mexico scheduled commitments according to the Understanding on Financial Services, although limitations apply
- all essentially undertook their commitments on a most favored nation basis

This synopsis masks some important differences among the OECD countries. Thus, branches are treated differently from subsidiaries in all OECD countries except

New Zealand and the United States. Australia, Canada, Switzerland, and the United States have inscribed in their schedules limitations on market access and national treatment for subnational regulation and monopolies in some types of insurance. As noted earlier, Japan used the additional commitments article to bind its bilateral agreements with the United States. The United States and the European Union promised greater efforts at internal regulatory harmonization via this same article.

Developing Countries and Transition Economies. In his study, Mattoo divided developing countries and transition economies into four geographical regions: Africa (forty-one countries), Asia and the Pacific (twenty-five countries), eastern Europe (seven countries), and Latin America, including the Caribbean (thirty-two countries). Notably, neither China nor Russia is a member. About one-half of the countries in Mattoo's study group, which account for 95 percent of the gross domestic product (GDP) of nondeveloped member countries, made commitments on direct insurance services. In both numerical and GDP-weighted terms, country participation was highest in eastern Europe, where all WTO members made commitments. Participation was lowest in Africa, where, of the forty-one WTO members, only thirteen made commitments (but these countries accounted for four-fifths of African members' GDP).

In Latin America, eighteen of the thirty-two member countries made commitments in insurance, with these eighteen countries accounting for 97 percent of the region's GDP. In Asia, seventeen of the twenty-five member countries made commitments in insurance, with the seventeen countries accounting for 25 percent of GDP of member countries in the region.

Participating countries differ significantly in the extent of their bindings and the restrictiveness of scheduled limitations. Full liberalization across the three major modes of supply is rare. Of fifty-two countries making commitments in direct insurance, only four small countries committed to full liberalization. Egypt and South Africa are the only two developing countries to guarantee an absence of restrictions on either of the two cross-border modes.

In each of the regions examined by Mattoo, commercial presence was clearly the mode through which members preferred to guarantee access to domestic markets for direct insurance services. As many as nineteen countries, accounting for almost 25 percent of participants' GDP, guaranteed the absence of restrictions (other than as to legal form) on commercial presence. Mattoo observed that, of the participant countries, eastern Europe as a region represents potentially the most liberal market for foreign investment in direct insurance.

Next in degree of openness is Africa, where seven of the thirteen countries making commitments imposed no restrictions on commercial presence, other than as to legal form. Nigeria and South Africa are included among the seven. Egypt, Gabon, and Mauritius apply economic-needs tests or discretionary procedures in allowing new entry, while Morocco includes a reciprocity condition in its schedule. Egypt, Ghana, and Kenya (in life insurance) impose equity limitations, but Ghana and Kenya already allow majority foreign ownership. Egypt limits foreign equity to 49 percent, but is raising the limit to 51 percent in the year 2000 for life and 2003 for nonlife insurance.

The number of assurances of fully open markets for foreign investors is higher in Asia and the Pacific (seven out of seventeen) than in Latin America (three of eighteen). Furthermore, several relatively large Asian markets (including Hong Kong, Indonesia, Israel, and Turkey, accounting for 32 percent of Asian participants' GDP) have no significant restrictions on the establishment of foreign commercial presence. The same can be said only for the smaller Latin American economies (Guyana, Panama, and Paraguay, accounting for only 1 percent of Latin American participants' GDP).

The nature of restrictions in the two regions reveals an interesting difference, according to Mattoo. He noted that the Latin group seems primarily reluctant to guarantee free entry, whereas the Asian group seems reluctant to assure full foreign ownership. In the Latin group, eleven members (including Argentina, Brazil, and Chile) do not assure fully liberal entry conditions. Two members (Cuba and Mexico) impose only equity limitations for entry, and another two countries (Dominican Republic and Honduras) do not assure liberal entry and impose equity limitations. In the Asian group, entry limitations are accompanied in eight cases (including India, Malaysia, Philippines, and Thailand) by restrictions on foreign equity as well. One member (Korea) imposes equity limitations only, whereas just one member (Qatar) imposes limitations on entry only. Mattoo observed that the contrast between regions may be less stark than it appears because the discretion Latin American countries retain to impose conditions on new entry could also apply to foreign equity participation.

Most developing countries and transition economies, as with the OECD countries, bound the status quo. A few countries bound at less than the status quo, including Korea, Malaysia, and Mexico. Some, including Brazil, Egypt, and most transition economies, effectively bound at greater than the status quo, inscribing future liberalization commitments as additional commitments.

A few countries' commitments were particularly disappointing. As mentioned, three large economies bound at less than the status quo, with Mexico and Korea failing to bind the level of their OECD commitments. Some commentators believe these failures were due more to the rush of final negotiations than to a lack of commitment to liberalization by these two countries. Malaysia's offers might be regarded as one of the most disappointing, given the level of its economic development and its insurance market. It did not "grandfather" access of existing insurance firms, did not provide for majority ownership for new entrants, and guaranteed little new market access. The other major disappointment was the failure of India to make any liberalization commitments in insurance, reflecting its inability to achieve national insurance reform at that time.

6

What More Is Needed?

That the GATS exists is, in itself, a great tribute to member countries. Yet more can be done to promote liberalization through both a more intensive application of traditional trade concepts and also innovative approaches to promoting competition. This section explores these issues.

Generic Improvements

Much has already been written about the perceived generic shortcomings of the GATS.[1] These shortcomings apply equally to insurance, but it seems redundant to delve deeply into them here. Let me merely note some of them briefly. First, to the extent possible, issues should be addressed across sectors rather than on a sector-by-sector basis; this will encourage consistency.

Second, the conditional positive list approach adopted in the GATS complicates attempts at interpreting, documenting, and measuring the benefits of liberalization achieved under the GATS.[2] It makes for potentially much less transparency, especially with respect to unbound sectors. The negative list approach would require all countries to perform extensive regulatory audits that then might permit better assessments of the contestability of their markets. As a practical matter, however, it seems unlikely negotiators will be able to restructure the agreement to rely on negative lists. Perhaps as the commitments of members strengthen over time, there will be less opposition to the change.

Another generic shortcoming of the GATS that applies to insurance is the absence of a standstill requirement, except for those countries scheduling commitments via the Understanding. This omission is unfortunate because it allows members actually to reduce their degree of liberalization and yet remain in compliance with the terms of the agreement. This flows from the use of the positive list approach for sectors or modes of supply that are unbound. Additionally, as mentioned above, some members scheduled their commitments at less than their regulatory status quo, which in theory permits backsliding.

The complex issues associated with government procurement, subsidies, and emergency safeguard measures are yet to be resolved. Each of these issues, especially the first two, is relevant for insurance.

Finally, there is the question of the interaction between the national-treatment obligation and modes of supply (Article I).[3] Article XVIII on national treatment makes no reference to modes of supply, unlike Article XVI on market access. At issue: do national-treatment obligations extend across all modes of supply, regardless of market-access commitments, or can members discriminate between identical services supplied via different modes? Of course, greater liberalization would flow from the former interpretation.

The balance of this chapter focuses on two aspects of the agreement that need substantial work: strengthening existing commitments and addressing nondiscriminatory regulatory barriers.

The Need to Strengthen Commitments

Aside from the possibility of strengthening the structure of the GATS, members need to bind more sectors and more modes of supply for each sector, and decrease the inscribed limits on commitments. Additionally, exemptions on most favored nation status for particular sectors that were taken by several members should be the object of negotiation.

The Need for Greater and Deeper Country Participation. As Mattoo reported, only about one-half of developing countries and transition economies have made commitments in insurance, although they include the major developing and transition economies. As a first order, insurance commitments should be secured from a greater number of countries.

Second, the commitments of developing countries to market access and, therefore, national treatment are neither strong nor extensive. Only about a quarter of member developing countries and transition economies made any commitments on market access, although some of the more economically advanced such countries are among this group. Among all countries making commitments, relatively few developing or developed countries fully bound the two cross-border modes. Market access via commercial presence was the predominant mode bound, although comparatively few developing countries made full commitments.

Third, more countries need to enter commitments via the Understanding. The Understanding generally requires more meaningful liberalization and has the advantage, because it employs the negative list approach, of minimizing misunderstanding.

No doubt several developing countries' reluctance to make strong commitments stemmed from concern that the quality of their insurance supervision was insufficient to oversee new competition adequately. Such concerns may be legitimate, although some countries have been accused of "foot dragging." The political and market power of established insurance interests can hinder liberalization. To the extent that the concern about regulatory supervision is legitimate, however, it is in the interests of the developed market economies to ensure that sufficient technical assistance is available to help developing countries make progress in regulatory effectiveness.

Among those developing countries making commitments to market access via commercial presence, many retained the right to impose limitations on the equity participation of foreign interests. Unlike the concern over regulatory capacity, such limits have no sound economic reasons. They are blatantly protectionistic.

Other inscribed commercial-presence limitations include ones related to legal form and others related to joint ventures. Economic-needs tests and numerical quotas are also found. These limitations, too, find weak economic justification at best and should be the object of negotiation for removal.

Stronger commitments to market access via the two cross-border delivery modes are desirable but problematic. Member countries' reluctance to bind these modes likely results from two concerns. First are the ever-present foreign exchange and national development worries of some developing countries, who fear cross-border insurance trade could exacerbate their foreign exchange problems and fail to assist them in building their national financial resources. The first concern is likely greatest in countries that maintain strict currency controls. The issues of currency control are larger than insurance, but they provide poor justification for restrictions on insurance trade. Additionally, forced localization requirements are second-best solutions at most.[4]

The second concern relates to consumer protection. This concern can be valid. Individuals and small businesses can be particularly ill-informed about insurance, which is why government regulation is typically more intensive where such consumers are involved than it is in transactions involving only large businesses. Protections of less-informed insurance buyers against more knowledgeable and occasionally even unscrupulous insurers can be thwarted if insurers are not subject to the laws and regulations of the country where the buyer lives, as happens in cross-border insurance trade. The evolution of electronic commerce will exacerbate this concern.

Given the broadness of the prudential carve-out in the GATS, it could be argued that much of the above concern falls within that article. Such an interpretation would presumably allow countries to show only limited reservations under the two market-access delivery modes for cross-border trade, while still maintaining substantial restrictions on that trade. This would be unfortunate for two reasons.

First, cross-border direct insurance that involves informed buyers, as with MAT insurance and insurance purchased by large corporations, needs little restriction. This same logic applies to reinsurance and retrocessions, to auxiliary insurance services, and possibly to insurance intermediation, depending on the types of insurance involved. Member governments could readily commit to liberalization of these areas, as several have through the Understanding.

Second, and more challenging, greater innovation under the terms of the GATS would permit cross-border insurance trade even for poorly informed buyers. This can be done through mutual regulatory recognition. Recall that provisions under the framework agreement and in the financial services annex allow recognition of prudential measures. These provisions can be the vehicles for greater liberalization. Additionally, this issue should be addressed in an electronic commerce context when issues associated with e-commerce more broadly are considered.

Finally, many WTO members explicitly breach the national-treatment principle in several ways. Special authorization requirements may apply exclusively to foreign insurers. Limitations on the ownership of land, and nationality and residency requirements for members of the board of directors, also are common. Taxation and subsidy issues have national-treatment implications. These and other national-treatment inconsistencies should be the object of negotiation. They find little or no justification in economic theory or practice.

Securing Meaningful Participation by Developing Countries. The benefits of liberalization in insurance do not differ fundamentally from those associated with trade in goods and in other services. Countries should willingly make unilateral liberalizing commitments if no meaningful consumer or market harm would ensue. But many developing countries appear to be either unconvinced of the benefits of liberalization or fearful that their regulatory capacities are insufficient to provide the needed structure for a competitive, liberalized market. A companion concern is that regulatory personnel are of insufficient quantity or quality to provide needed oversight, even with appropriate laws and regulations. The solution would be a deeper commitment by developed countries to technical assistance so as to ensure developing countries have the necessary infrastructure to regulate effectively.

In addition, some already liberal OECD countries worry that the traditional offer-acceptance negotiating process which proceeds by reciprocal (incorrectly termed) "concessions" will prove less effective for the next round of negotiations. What concessions can an already liberal market exchange for concessions from an illiberal market? Where is the demanders' leverage in circumstances in which cross-sector trade-offs are not permitted?

Perhaps more empirical evidence is needed on the benefits of insurance liberalization. We have theoretical and limited anecdotal evidence,[5] but little by way of empirical support. Given the limitations on data, any such studies will be far from perfect, but they could be helpful.

Nondiscriminatory Regulatory Barriers

The case for governmental intervention into insurance markets is soundly grounded in economic theory. Intervention can rectify problems stemming from market failures, three of which are paramount in financial services: market power, externalities, and information problems. No two countries, even within the European Union, follow the same approach to addressing these problems, and it seems unwise to try to force countries to do so. The unique cultural, economic, political, and historical circumstances of every country argue for each crafting its insurance regulation to fit those circumstances. Herein lies a challenge for enhancing the contestability of national insurance markets via international trade.

Ordinarily that challenge is less relevant for trade in goods, because international trade in goods and in services exhibits some important differences, as table 6-1 shows. These differences collectively explain why it is often possible to separate domestic regulatory issues from trade measures in goods but not in insurance and other financial services.

The control of international trade in goods relies heavily on at-the-border measures, while the control of trade in financial services relies more on behind-the-border measures by domestic regulators. This means trade negotiations for financial services are generally more complex than those for goods.

The Case for Deeper Integration. Regulation that appears purely domestic can become an unfair and often unintentional barrier to trade in insurance services in two ways.

Table 6-1 Important Differences Between International Trade in Goods and in Insurance

Characteristic	International Trade in Goods	International Trade in Insurance
Tradable?	Yes	No
Reasonably transparent pricing?	Yes, because tradable	No, because not tradable and products are complex
Linkage as input to other production clearly understood?	Yes	No, complicated by product complexity, with few analyses existing
Subject to tariffs or tariffication?	Yes	No
International trade may require establishment?	No, with exceptions	Yes
Dependent on local factor inputs?	No	Yes, if via establishment
Subject to potentially severe market-failure problems?	No, except for health and safety issues	Yes, especially for individuals and small-business purchasers

First, differences in regulation between countries can themselves hinder global competition in insurance services by (1) magnifying the negative effects of market failures, (2) provoking more stringent domestic trade-related regulation, and (3) increasing transactional costs.[6] Applying the national-treatment standard does not resolve these difficulties.

Second, regardless of any international differences in regulation, some regulatory practices unnecessarily hinder effective market access and tilt the competitive balance in favor of established firms vis-à-vis new entrants. The national-treatment standard is insufficient to address these problems. National-treatment barriers to market access exist when governments restrict the number of competitors within their markets, limit distribution systems, strictly regulate insurance products or rates such that foreign innovators are hindered in exploiting their competitive advantage, and, in general, whenever restrictive government regulation provides existing (usually mostly national) firms an advantage over potential entrants. The same restrictive result can obtain when established competitors enjoy market power because of a failure of government to regulate competition effectively. In other words, both overly restrictive and inadequate regulation can unduly restrain the contestability of a nation's market.

Improvements in commitments or in the structure of the agreement will not meaningfully address these two classes of regulatory issues. Thus, firms from different countries may not enjoy comparable levels of market access under traditional trade policy instruments. This is especially likely the more the countries differ in their regulatory schemes, especially in industries like insurance that receive intensive regulation. One solution to this problem is regulatory convergence.

Regulatory Convergence and Mutual Recognition. Regulatory convergence could come about from government-initiated moves to harmonize relevant laws and regulations, or it could evolve if disparate market participants cajole their governments to seek common regulatory approaches. Countries could make their relevant laws and regulations mirror images of each other (*de jure* harmonization), or harmonization could focus more on the quality of regulation (*de facto* harmonization), with relevant laws and regulations being, in substance, equivalent to each other without being identical. Either way, the quality and nature of enforcement are as critical as the laws and regulations themselves.

No compelling economic evidence suggests that broad-based, *de jure* regulatory harmonization would result in greater liberalization of insurance markets worldwide.[7] Unlike the situation with banks, market failures in insurance seem unlikely to pose important risks to a nation's financial system and especially to the international financial system— risks that prudential harmonization might reduce. Prosperous, liberalized national insurance markets function efficiently in many insurance lines without forced harmonization. The existing level of economic knowledge argues against harmonization.

Instead, the key to further liberalization of international insurance seems to lie in mutual regulatory recognition. If one nation believes that another affords the first nation's insurance consumers adequate protection, regardless of how it does it, the first nation arguably should be content with the second's regulation, and vice versa. Although unilateral recognition would suffice to liberalize a country's market, the more politically appealing approach is mutual recognition.

Transparency is critical for the success of mutual recognition. Among other things, transparency is meant to ensure that home-country regulators and insurers are informed about the rules and regulations of the host-country. This transparency is necessary for effective market access and operation by foreigners. Transparency also runs in the other direction: it is meant to ensure that host-country regulators are informed about the effectiveness of home-country regulation. Such transparency is justified on prudential and consumer protection grounds.

Both types of transparency require substantial cross-national regulatory communication, coordination, and cooperation. Notice, comment, due process, and publication requirements reinforce transparency.

Implicit within the goal of transparency is a high level of interjurisdictional trust. National regulators must be confident that their international counterparts are dealing openly and honestly with them before they will agree to mutual recognition. This will become even more important as e-commerce continues to penetrate markets. Organizations such as the International Association of Insurance Supervisors (IAIS) and the OECD appear to have important roles here.

Confidence-building measures akin to those of the U.S. accreditation program of the National Association of Insurance Commissioners could be appealing, but implementation would be daunting. If some minimal *de facto* regulatory harmonization proved politically useful for building confidence, the IAIS would be a logical locus for the effort. Alternatively, like-minded countries could agree to appropriate harmonization, in which case the OECD might be a good focal point.

Mutual recognition, instead of national treatment, can mean better treatment for foreign firms if the home country's rules are superior to those of the host country. Permitting such regulatory competition could set in motion a continuous process of regulatory Darwinism that would lead to market-driven regulatory convergence.

Procompetitive Regulatory Principles for Insurance

The December 1997 Agreement can be made more responsive to contemporary policy problems, which can be summarized as follows:

- Diverse national regulation, predicated on the outdated assumption of discrete, insular national economies, hinders global competition in financial services.
- Many regulatory practices unnecessarily hinder effective market access and tilt the competitive balance in favor of established firms over new entrants.

• Traditional trade policy principles are insufficient because most such principles are ill-suited to address the new generation of regulatory issues.

The new order of global competition has thus revealed problems with existing regulatory and trade policy approaches. This results in imbalances that hinder and distort competition.

Perhaps the next step to structuring insurance markets that will better serve each country's interest should be regulatory reform built on a set of procompetitive regulatory principles designed to ensure competitive, solvent, and fair markets. A paper prepared for the U.S. Coalition of Service Industries offers a set of general principles,[8] summarized and discussed briefly below, that are consistent with the GATS Article VI.

These principles could move national insurance markets toward the competitive ideal, but they are not an argument for eliminating regulation. In fact, procompetitive regulation requires a greater, not lesser emphasis on solvency oversight, transparency and consumer information, and market monitoring. An insurance market structured on these principles will have regulation that is adequate, impartial, minimally intrusive, and, importantly, transparent.

These principles, like those of the telecommunications annex, could form the basis for permitting deeper and more uniform integration in insurance while ensuring adequate consumer protection. Each country's insurance regulation could be subject to analysis against these principles, as part of the negotiation process. Ultimately, more specificity may be desirable, perhaps through the International Association of Insurance Supervisors. But the establishment of greater specificity, such as setting regulatory standards, would be outside the scope of the World Trade Organization's mandate.

To promote the twin goals of a competitive and solvent insurance market, insurance regulation should be

- adequate
- impartial
- minimally intrusive
- transparent

Each area is addressed below, with appropriate pro-competitive regulatory principles offered. These principles can serve as the basis for building competitive insurance markets that serve the best interest of each country's citizens.

Regulation Should Be Adequate. Regulation should be adequate, meaning it should be able to rectify meaningful market failures and protect the public. Several principles of adequacy follow.

Competition law. To establish an adequate system of regulation, governments must first have necessary laws and regulations in place that create the framework for a competitive market. Our first principle, therefore, is, *Governments should enact and enforce laws that provide an effective framework for competitive insurance markets.*

Competition (or antitrust) law is a vital component of this framework. Such law regulates the nature of competition in the marketplace rather than individual competitors. As markets move from restrictive to liberal regulatory approaches, competition law becomes more important because some firms will have motives to engage in anticompetitive practices. The law should give regulators clear authority to prevent or punish collective behavior that lessens competition, such as collusive price setting, market-sharing arrangements, and other anticompetitive collective actions.

Article IX of the GATS touches on this principle, but it imposes no obligations on members beyond consultation. More is needed.

Prudential regulation. Insurance laws and regulations should also address all relevant aspects of insurer operations, from creation to liquidation. The most important component involves prudential regulation and supervision, which brings us to the next principle related to adequate regulation: *Governments should enact laws that establish reasonable solvency standards and regulation as the primary means of protecting the public.*

The more competitive a market, the more important prudential regulation and accompanying supervision are. The insurance regulator in a deregulated market faces more difficult issues than his counterpart in a strictly regulated market. Indeed, prudential regulation and supervision can be deceptively simple in markets in which all insurers charge the same or similar prices, which allows even the least efficient insurer to earn profits. Insolvencies in such markets are diminished by overcharging, a form of pre-insolvency assessment.

Not all insolvencies can or should be prevented. In a competitive market, some insolvencies are inevitable. Government's delicate task is to minimize the harm to consumers produced by such difficulties without signaling other insurers that mismanagement or other unsound business practices will be tolerated. Rigorous but fair enforcement of well-crafted prudential regulation is required.

The emphasis of prudential regulation and supervision should be to prevent insurers from incurring excessive levels of financial risk and to intervene in a timely way when an insurer's financial condition becomes hazardous. This can be accomplished by reasonable minimum financial standards and effective monitoring of insurers' financial conditions. Such a strategy should include frequent informal consultations with insurer executives to keep regulators well informed about potentially adverse developments and to enable them to steer insurers away from actions that threaten policyholders' interests.

Resolving the problems of financial difficulties for existing insurers should be a priority. Thus, our next principle: *As a part of reasonable solvency regulation, governments should make public, and enforce, consistent rules and procedures for identifying and dealing with financially troubled insurers.*

Insurance regulation should aim to establish incentives for efficient and safe operation by insurers and to institute safeguards that keep insurer insolvencies to an acceptable minimum. A marketplace with no insurer failures is likely to be one in which insurance is expensive and consumer choice is limited.

Government's responsibility is to establish rules and procedures for identifying and dealing with financially troubled insurers. A key element in the identification process is the establishment of appropriate accounting, reporting, and auditing standards and requirements. Governments would be wise to borrow freely from international best-practices standards.

The rules for dealing with troubled insurers should address the particular difficulty and be consistently applied across all competitors. The rules and procedures should be made public and any changes subject to transparent regulatory processes (see below).

The GATS prudential carve-out—a needed inclusion—is broadly worded. As such, it could be the basis for countries' effectively nullifying some of their obligations. The challenge for regulators and trade officials will be how best to interpret both the carve-out and this principle in a way all parties can accept.

Regulatory effectiveness. To ensure adequate regulation in a competitive market, *Governments should establish an insurance regulatory agency that operates in society's interest and has sufficient resources to efficiently, effectively, and impartially enforce the nation's insurance laws and regulations.*

If the agency is to function in society's interests, as opposed to private interests, it should operate independently of undue insurance industry and other special-interest influence. It is not enough to have the regulatory body be a government agency. The means by which industry input is secured must be transparent, impartial, and consistent. Rules may be necessary to limit undue influence over regulatory decisions; for example, former heads of the regulatory agency may be forbidden to lobby the agency for a certain time after vacating the office. Due process and transparency are critical to ensuring that the regulator deals at arm's length with the regulated.

The regulatory body must be provided sufficient financial and other resources, including information technology, to carry out its regulatory function. The quality and integrity of supervisory personnel are crucial. Because regulation in competitive markets is more complex than regulation in restrictive markets, a competitive market requires highly skilled regulatory employees.

Regulatory *efficiency* means that responsibilities are carried out expeditiously, with prudent use of the agency's resources. Regulatory *effectiveness* means that responsibilities are carried out in ways that genuinely ameliorate the identified market failure, using approaches that are minimally intrusive. Regulatory *impartiality* means that responsibilities are carried out with fairness to all market participants. Impartiality is so important it warrants separate treatment below.

Phased-in liberalization.   In many emerging market-economy countries, regulatory oversight of insurance may not be sufficiently attuned to protecting consumers in a competitive market. As the experience of several Latin American countries attests, these countries may need to enhance prudential, competition, and market-conduct regulation and supervision as they reregulate and liberalize their insurance markets. At the same time, the movement from a restrictive to a competitive market does not take place overnight, which brings us to our next principle: *Governments should develop insurance regulations that enhance competition in a way that ensures adequate protection of the public but proceeds without undue delay, subject to a reasonable implementation timetable.*

New insurer entry into formerly restrictive markets should not be allowed to overwhelm government's ability to protect both consumers and the stability of the national insurance industry. On the other hand, experience suggests that concerns about consumer protection are often asserted to justify unreasonable delays in liberalizing. Policymakers should recognize that entrenched interests will always urge slowness in reform. Yet the road to reform should be traveled at the maximum possible *safe* speed, not the minimum. Reform should follow a carefully crafted route, which means that an implementation timetable, with clear deadlines, is essential.

Regulation Should Be Impartial. The principle of impartiality is fundamental to a competitive market. Governments should accord no competitor or group of competitors more favorable treatment than that extended to other competitors or groups of competitors. Thus, our next procompetitive regulatory principle is, *Governments should apply insurance regulation and enforcement consistently and impartially between competitors, regardless of nationality.*

Historically, the fair trade principle of national treatment, found in the GATS Article XVII, has been the standard for impartiality, and this standard is a reasonable test of impartiality in minimally intrusive regulatory regimes, where it ensures equality of opportunity for foreign entrants

Additionally, the GATS Article VI on Domestic Regulation has an impartiality requirement, but only with respect to inscribed commitments.

National-treatment problems exist for foreign insurers in some markets. Thus, some countries have different deposit or capital requirements for foreign insurers than for national ones. Many countries assess higher taxes on foreign than on national insurers. Some countries deny or restrict membership in local trade associations for foreign insurers, denying them equal access to national statistics, research, and lobbying.

As I noted earlier, the national-treatment standard is insufficient to ensure effective market access under certain circumstances. Other government actions that can distort the competitive balance include exchange controls, deposit and lending-rate ceilings, privileged access to credit, and unnecessarily strict controls on investments and business powers. Such strict regulation affords already established firms a competitive advantage over new entrants.

Regulation Should Be Minimally Intrusive. All insurance regulation should aim at rectifying meaningful market failures, that is, to protect the public interest. A government has multiple ways of rectifying each imperfection it identifies. All of the ways may meet the adequacy test in the sense that they suffice to accomplish the purpose. Some means, however, will disrupt the competitive market less than others, while still accomplishing their purpose. In selecting among its many options, governments should choose those that accomplish the purpose with minimal disruption to the smooth functioning of their insurance markets; in trade terms, government should select among those that are the least trade restrictive (that is, that meet a "necessity test"). Government should avoid regulating matters with little or no possibility of harming the public. Thus, an important procompetitive regulatory principle is, *Insurance regulation should be limited to that which is (1) justified by providing meaningful protection and (2) minimally intrusive to accomplish its purpose.* This is the principle embedded in the GATS Article VI requirement that measures should be no more burdensome than necessary to ensure the quality of the service. Of course, the requirement applies only to specific commitments.

This philosophy implies that insurers should be allowed to offer an array of insurance products at prices they deem appropriate, without being subject to severe restrictions or a cumbersome pre-approval process, unless meaningful consumer harm could result from doing so. Market forces should prevent insurers from sustaining prices above a competitive level. Insurers that charge inadequate prices or incur excessive financial risk can be removed from the market. Products that do not serve consumer needs also will not be viable. Through effective monitoring and actions, regulators should move decisively against insurers that attempt to defraud consumers or treat them unfairly. The threat of timely regulatory enforcement actions and appropriate penalties will help to discourage insurers and intermediaries from engaging in abusive practices. This approach conserves regulatory resources by directing them toward the small number of insurers and intermediaries that treat consumers unfairly, without subjecting all market participants to unnecessary constraints or burdensome oversight.

An important element of the minimally intrusive principle is having the government act to increase corporate accountability without government itself being responsible for the details of oversight. Thus, requiring audits and certifications by independent actuaries and accountants can both relieve government of these tasks and create positive incentives for insurers. Placing more responsibility on management and boards of directors can have similar effects. The importance of "fit and proper" standards for key management grows with greater market competition.

I would stress that the standard of minimal intrusion does not imply a policy of laissez faire or no regulatory oversight. Rather, it implies that regulation should be confined to interventions that are truly needed and can meaningfully benefit consumers. Effective regulatory monitoring can help to ensure that regulators are alerted to problems that require action on a timely basis.

When determining regulations, policymakers and regulators must consider the frequency and severity of market abuses and problems. It is not feasible to prevent consumers from ever making poor choices. Government should focus on areas where there is a pattern of abuse or practices harmful to consumers that reflect fundamental gaps in consumers' abilities to protect themselves.

Distribution and product regulation. Restrictive markets usually exist under the philosophy that insurers may do only that which is expressly authorized beforehand by regulators. Such a scheme of regulation can ensure a stable market, but such markets are rarely innovative, typically offer high-priced insurance, and provide comparatively limited consumer choice and value. Thus, consistent with the minimally intrusive standard, our next principle is, *Subject only to regulatory oversight that is essential to protect the public, governments should allow the market to determine (1) what financial services products should be developed and sold, (2) the methods by which they will be sold, and (3) the prices at which they will be sold.*

Deregulation connotes a lessening of national regulation with the goal of retaining only what is adequate and minimally intrusive. The critical first step toward reasoned deregulation is to adopt the philosophy that insurers should have the flexibility to respond to consumer needs in ways *they* deem appropriate, subject to regulatory oversight to deal with solvency matters and to minimize misleading or abusive practices. Market forces will encourage insurers to develop and sell products on terms that are in the best interest of consumers.

This approach argues for greater reliance on after-the-fact oversight, wherever it is most efficient. Before-the-fact regulation will remain appropriate for some areas, such as insurer licensing and solvency oversight, where certain market failures are best addressed by imposing minimum standards and prohibiting activities that could harm consumers, such as situations where lack of information and unequal bargaining power between consumers and insurers can lead to abuses.

Many countries have shifted more to after-the-fact regulation. Even so, remnants of earlier restrictive approaches persist, if not strictly in law then at least in practice. The product approval process in many countries is at best sluggish and at worst erratic, arbitrary, and opaque. The benefits of competition—product innovation, the adjustment of prices, and the like—are blunted when regulation is slow, unpredictable, or inconsistent.

A competitive insurance market will have numerous channels for insurance distribution. New products and services require channels attuned to the buyer's needs and wishes. Brokers and other marketing intermediaries can help insurance buyers make better informed decisions. Government-imposed limitations on distribution channels that could serve the market more efficiently are inconsistent with a market-driven regulatory philosophy. They are examples of governmentally created barriers to entry.

Disclosure and consumer information. When a government moves from a restrictive regulatory system to greater reliance on competition, some consumer-protection functions shift from the government to consumers themselves. Government should make sure insurance buyers understand that such a fundamental shift has taken place because buyers will need to become more active in evaluating insurers and their products. This brings us to our next principle: *Governments should make certain that insurance customers have access to sufficient information to enable them to make informed, independent judgments as to (1) an insurer's financial condition and (2) the value of its products.*

Regulation may be necessary to compel insurers to make certain disclosures in connection with their marketing. In other instances, it may be most effective for government itself to be the source of needed, unbiased information, although this will require additional governmental efforts to facilitate informed customer choices.

Rating agencies and other independent information sources can greatly assist customers as sources of unbiased information. Unfortunately, some governments discourage or prohibit entry by rating agencies and other such independent financial service information firms. Such actions hinder competition by denying local businesses and citizens information that they need regarding the purchase and maintenance of insurance and other financial service products.

The Regulatory Process Should Be Transparent. A transparent regulatory process is fundamental to ensuring a competitive market. This brings us to two of the most important procompetitive regulatory principles. The first is, *Governments should make existing insurance laws and regulations easily available to the public, including to consumers and businesses and to insurers and other providers of financial services.*

The fair trade principle of transparency, as embedded in the GATS Article III, requires that regulatory and other legal requirements regarding market access and national operation should be clearly and fully set out and easily available. Transparency problems are too common in insurance markets. Many governments' laws and regulations are not readily available. Foreign firms, in particular, encounter transparency problems in countries that grant their regulators broad discretionary powers, as the foreign insurer may have no clear understanding of the market access or operational requirements.

Many countries, especially those that historically have been relatively closed, may have unclear or nonexistent standards of due process. In such instances, foreign (and national) insurers may not fully understand either their rights to appeal regulatory decisions or the process by which an appeal is undertaken.

The second dimension of the transparency principle applies to proposed laws and regulations. This dimension requires that all interested parties have the opportunity to know about and to comment on proposed regulations and that challenges to regulatory decisions be possible. Transparency, then, requires a second regulatory principle: *When crafting proposed insurance laws and regulations, governments should (1) make such proposals easily available to the public, (2) invite comment on the proposals, (3) allow sufficient time for interested parties to provide comment, (4) provide justifications for decisions to accept and reject comments, and (5) establish a fair process by which decisions can be challenged.*

Although impressive gains in transparency have been made in many markets, others continue to draw criticism internationally. Close relationships between government and established insurers are inconsistent with the ideal of transparency. Transparency implies that regulators maintain an arm's-length relationship with all insurers and that some insurers do not gain an unfair advantage through privileged associations with regulators.

7
Conclusion

The GATS represents a major advance in free trade by providing a structure for international trade in insurance services. Yet more can and should be done.

Besides the desirability of making some structural changes in the agreement, broader and deeper commitments are needed. Success in achieving this objective, however, will not suffice. Still more is needed to ensure liberal, competitive markets.

The internationalization of financial services promises to continue. This new order of global business has revealed gaps in existing regulatory and trade policy approaches. The result is competitive imbalances that hinder and distort global competition. The policy question is how to continue to promote competition through liberalization under the GATS while ensuring adequate consumer protection.

Divergent national regulatory approaches caused fewer difficulties when financial services markets were insulated from each other and largely domestic. For the future, however, overly restrictive regulation can impede the continued internationalization of financial services. Many observers believe that regulatory convergence will evolve. If so, it should be market driven, with attempts by governments to impose harmonization avoided.

Some observers express concern about the competitive model, given the recent economic turmoil experienced in several countries. But competition itself did not cause the difficulties. Rather, the lack of certain government rules and policies inhibited truly transparent, competitive markets and made a bad situation much worse. Some argue that greater market access and involvement by foreign financial services firms would have lessened the adverse economic effects. The lesson for governments is to craft laws and enforce regulations that promote more transparent markets, supported by fair competition that is unfettered by government direction, favoritism, and unwarranted interference.

Competitive insurance markets serve each country's interest. Governments that deny their citizens and businesses such markets lessen consumer choice and value and needlessly hinder national economic development.

The challenge for the GATS in insurance is how to move to greater integration. Further change could best follow the lead of the telecommunications sector by embedding a set of procompetitive regulatory principles within the GATS. These principles can form the basis for creating competitive insurance markets in the public interest. The details of implementation will vary from market to market according to each country's particular circumstances. If the implementation details are consistent with the principles, however, governments will have unleashed the great power of the market for the benefit of their citizens and economies.

Notes

Chapter 2: An Overview of Insurance and Insurance Markets

1. This section draws liberally from Harold D. Skipper, Jr., *International Risk and Insurance: An Environmental-Managerial Approach* (Boston: Irwin McGraw-Hill, 1998), chaps. 1 and 4.
2. All data are from *sigma*, no. 3 (1999), published by the global reinsurer Swiss Re.
3. The data source follows the European convention of including health and accident premiums in the nonlife category.
4. The Japanese insurance market actually is larger than suggested by this figure, probably larger than that of the United States. The data source did not include Kampo or Zenkyoren premium writings in its Japanese premium figures. Kampo is affiliated with the Japanese Post Office, through which its policies are sold. Zenkyoren are agricultural cooperative insurers. In 1997, Kampo had a 30.4 percent share of the Japanese life market, and Zenkyoren had a 14.7 percent share of the nonlife market. See *sigma*, no. 3 (1999): 14.
5. See Harold D. Skipper, Jr., *International Risk and Insurance: An Environmental-Managerial Approach*, chap. 4, for a summary of the studies on insurance demand and supply.
6. In the United States, a *domestic insurer* refers to one domiciled in the same state in which it sells insurance. A *foreign insurer* is one domiciled in a U.S. state different from that in which it sells insurance. An *alien insurer* is one domiciled in a country other than America.

Chapter 3: The Role of Insurance in Economic Development

1. This section draws from Harold D. Skipper, Jr., *Foreign Insurers in Emerging Markets: Issues and Concerns* (Washington, D.C.: International Insurance Foundation, 1997), 6–14.
2. Doocheol Kim, *The Determinants of Life Insurance Growth in Developing Countries, with Particular Reference to the Republic of Korea,* unpublished Ph.D. dissertation, Georgia State University (1988); and Swiss Reinsurance Company, "A Comparison of Social and Private Insurance, 1970–1985, in Ten Countries," *sigma* (1987).
3. International Monetary Fund, *World Economic Outlook: May 1995* (Washington, D.C., 1995), 69–70. Of course, this finding does not suggest that every country with a high savings rate will have a high growth rate. Countries whose financial systems are inefficient are less likely to achieve high growth rates even with high savings rates.

Chapter 4: Overview of the GATS

1. Other general obligations relate to anticompetitive business practices, economic integration agreements, and recognition of standards for authorization, licensing, or certification.
2. See, for example, Sydney J. Key, *Financial Services in the Uruguay Round and the WTO* (Washington, D.C.: Group of Thirty, 1997), 14–16.
3. The designation "unbound" means that no commitment is technically feasible.
4. For an excellent overview of this issue, see R. Brian Woodrow, "The World Trade Organization Accord and Liberalization of Trade in Insurance Services: Impact and Implications of the 1995 Protocol on Financial Services," *Geneva Papers on Risk and Insurance: Issues and Practice,* no. 84 (July 1997).

Chapter 5: What the GATS Has Accomplished in Insurance

1. Aaditya Mattoo, "Financial Services and the WTO: Liberalization in the Developing and Transition Economies," preliminary draft, and R. Brian Woodrow, "The World Trade Organization Accord and Liberalization of Trade in Insurance Services: Impact and Implications of the 1995 Protocol on Financial Services," *Geneva Papers on Risk and Insurance: Issues and Practice,* no. 84 (July 1997).

Chapter 6: What More Is Needed?

1. See, for example, Sydney J. Key, *Financial Services in the Uruguay Round and the WTO* (Washington, D.C.: Group of Thirty, 1997).

2. Pierre Sauvé, "Services and the International Contestability of Markets" (Paris: OECD Trade Directorate, n.d.), 7.

3. Other important national treatment issues exist. See, for example, Aaditya Mattoo, "National Treatment in the GATS: Corner-stone or Pandora's Box" (Geneva: World Trade Organization, January 22, 1997).

4. Harold D. Skipper, Jr., *Foreign Insurers in Emerging Markets: Issues and Concerns* (Washington, D.C.: International Insurance Foundation, 1997), 2–4.

5. See, for example, Skipper, *Foreign Insurers in Emerging Markets.*

6. For a discussion of these three items, see Harold D. Skipper, Jr., "Regulatory Harmonization and Mutual Recognition in Insurance," in Harold D. Skipper, Jr., ed., *International Risk and Insurance: An Environmental-Managerial Approach,* chap. 14.

7. See, for example, Harold D. Skipper, Jr., "International Trade in Insurance," in Claude E. Barfield, ed., *International Financial Markets: Harmonization versus Competition* (Washington, D.C.: AEI Press, 1996), 151–223.

8. These principles and much of the narrative that follows are from Harold D. Skipper, Jr. and Robert W. Klein, "Insurance Regulation in the Public Interest: The Path towards Competitive, Solvent Markets," *Geneva Papers on Risk* and *Insurance: Issues and Practice* 25, no. 4 (October 2000).

About the Author

HAROLD D. SKIPPER, JR., is the C. V. Starr Chair of International Insurance at Georgia State University, where he is chairman of the department of risk management and insurance. His nonacademic experience includes serving as an economics affairs officer with the United Nations in Geneva and as consultant to regulators and intergovernmental organizations. He has been a visiting professor at the University of Paris and at Nanyang Technological University in Singapore. He is past president of the American Risk and Insurance Association and past vice president of the International Insurance Society. He serves on the boards of several organizations, including the Asia-Pacific Risk and Insurance Association and the advisory boards of financial services to the University of Beijing and to the Indian Institute of Management Bangalore. Besides several dozen articles, his publications include the books *International Risk and Insurance: An Environmental-Managerial Approach and Life Health Insurance.*